Contents

Authorised for experimental use under Canon XXII.4 *on behalf of the College of Bishops of the Scottish Episcopal Church.*

✠ *Edward Brechin* **Primus**

March 1988

Permission to reproduce the two Collects on pages 14 *and* 26 *kindly given by Taizé Community, from their* 'Praise in all our Days', *published by The Faith Press Ltd, Leighton Buzzard, Beds* LU7 7NQ.

ISBN 0 905573 07 2.

Introduction

The simple forms of morning and evening prayer given here are designed to encourage attentive prayer, either by groups or by individuals. The words are few, and are meant to be repeated slowly, quietly and reflectively, so that they may become part of us and may give voice to our own prayer.

Our prayer becomes the prayer of Christ's people: Christ's people's prayer becomes our prayer.

Ample opportunity should be taken for silence. Silence allows Christ's words to touch and to mingle with the thoughts of our hearts.

It has always been the Christian custom to pray with Christ at the beginning and at the end of each day:

The morning is the time of his resurrection: as the new light breaks we pray to be made new in him.

The evening is the time of his descent from the cross: as the sun sets we pray to find our final rest in him.

Even if we are insulated from the natural rhythm of dawn and dusk, as many these days are by patterns of work and family life, let our prayer fit the hymn:

'With thee began, with thee shall end the day'

as a sign that we seek to place all that we are, all that we say, and all that we do within the unending praise of the God and Father of our Lord Jesus Christ.

The structure of these simple forms is as follows:

I. A short invocation – calling upon God
   (in the morning from Psalm 51, in the evening from Psalm 70)

Gloria – praise of the God who through Jesus invites us to worship him as Father, Son, and Holy Spirit.

II. A psalm, followed by a short reading from scripture. (These vary according to the season.)

III. A canticle (in the morning **Benedictus,** in the evening **Magnificat**).

Short prayers, including the Lord's Prayer.

This structure is a very ancient one and has therefore been tested through long Christian experience. It is offered here in simple form in the hope that it may encourage all who use it to 'keep on praying and not to lose heart'.

Morning Prayer

I. INVOCATION

V O Lord open our lips;
R and our mouths shall proclaim your praise.

Glory to the Father, and the Son, and to the Holy Spirit:
as it was in the beginning is now, and shall be for ever. **AMEN.**

Now turn to pages 4, 5, 6, 7, 8, 9, 10, 11 or 12, according to the season.

II. PSALMODY AND SCRIPTURE

Advent (Anticipation)

Psalm 97

1. The Lord is king; let the earth rejoice:
   let the multitude of islands be glad.

2. Clouds and darkness are round about him:
   righteousness and justice are the foundation of his throne.

3. For you, Lord, are most high over all the earth:
   you are exalted far above all gods.

4. The Lord loves those that hate evil:
   the Lord guards the life of the faithful, and delivers them
      from the hand of the ungodly.

5. Light dawns for the righteous:
   and joy for the true of heart.

6. Rejoice in the Lord, you righteous:
   and give thanks to his holy name.

   Glory to the Father . . .

Besides this you know what hour it is, how it is full time now for you
to wake from sleep. For salvation is nearer to us now than when we
first believed. (Rom. 13.11 – 12)

Now turn to page 13

Christmas (Incarnation)

Psalm 98

1. O sing to the Lord a new song:
   for he has done marvellous things;

2. his right hand and his holy arm:
   they have got him the victory.

3. The Lord has made known his salvation:
   he has revealed his just deliverance in the sight of the
        nations.

4. He has remembered his mercy and faithfulness
        towards the house of Israel:
   and all the ends of the earth have seen
        the salvation of our God.

5. Shout with joy to the Lord, all the earth:
   break into singing and make melody.

6. For he comes to judge the earth:
   he shall judge the world with righteousness,
        and the peoples with equity.

   Glory to the Father . . .

In many and various ways God spoke of old to our fathers by the
prophets; but in these last days he has spoken to us by a Son, whom
he has appointed the heir of all things, through whom he also
created the world. (Heb. 1.1 − 2)

Now turn to page 13

Lent (Returning to God)

Psalm 51

1. Have mercy on me, O God, in your enduring goodness:
   according to the fulness of your compassion
      blot out my offences.

2. Wash me thoroughly from my wickedness:
   and cleanse me from my sin.

3. For I acknowledge my rebellion:
   and my sin is ever before me.

4. Create in me a clean heart, O God:
   and renew a right spirit within me.

5. Do not cast me out from your presence:
   do not take your holy spirit from me.

6. O give me the gladness of your help again:
   and support me with a willing spirit.

7. The sacrifice of God is a broken spirit:
   a broken and contrite heart, O God, you will not despise.

   Glory to the Father . . .

Finally, brethren, we beseech and exhort you in the Lord Jesus, that as you learned from us how you ought to live and to please God, just as you are doing, you do so more and more. For God has not called us for uncleaness, but in holiness. (1 Thess 4. 1, 7)

Now turn to page 13

Easter (Resurrection)

Psalm 150

1. Praise the Lord. O praise God in his sanctuary:
   praise him in the firmament of his power.

2. Praise him for his mighty acts:
   praise him according to his abundant goodness.

3. Praise him in the blast of the ram's horn:
   praise him upon the lute and harp.

4. Praise him with the timbrel and dances:
   praise him upon the strings and pipe.

5. Praise him on the high-sounding cymbals:
   praise him upon the loud cymbals.

6. Let everything that has breath praise the Lord:
   O praise the Lord!

   Glory to the Father . . .

God raised Jesus on the third day and made him manifest; not to all
the people but to us who were chosen by God as witnesses, who ate
and drank with him after he rose from the dead. (Acts 10.40 – 41)

Now turn to page 13

Ascension to Pentecost (Fulfilment)

Psalm 104

1. Bless the Lord, O my soul:
   O Lord my God, how great you are.

2. Clothed with majesty and honour:
   wrapped in light as in a garment.

3. You make the winds your messengers:
   and flames of fire your ministers.

4. Lord, how various are your works:
   in wisdom you have made them all, and the earth is full of
        your creatures.

5. When you send forth your spirit they are created:
   and you renew the face of the earth.

6. May the glory of the Lord endure for ever:
   may the Lord rejoice in his works.

   Glory to the Father . . .

The God of our fathers raised Jesus whom you killed by hanging
him on a tree. God exalted him at his right hand as Leader and
Saviour, to give repentance to Israel and forgiveness of sins. And we
are witnesses to these things, and so is the Holy Spirit whom God
has given to those who obey Him. (Acts 5.30 – 32)

Now turn to page 13

Other days

Option 1. *Psalm* 43

1. Give judgement for me O God,
      take up my cause against an ungodly people:
   deliver me from deceitful and wicked men.

2. For you are God my refuge, why have you turned me away:
   why must I go like a mourner because the enemy
      oppresses me ?

3. O send out your light and your truth and let them lead me:
   let them guide me to your holy hill and to your dwelling.

4. Then I shall go to the altar of God,
      to God my joy and my delight:
   and to the harp I shall sing your praises O God my God.

5. Why are you so full of heaviness my soul:
   and why so unquiet within me ?

6. O put your trust in God:
   for I will praise him yet who is my deliverer and my God.

   Glory to the Father . . .

The Lord's true love is surely not spent, nor has his compassion
failed; they are new every morning, so great is his constancy. The
Lord, I say, is all that I have; therefore I will wait for him patiently.
The Lord is good to those who look for him, to all who seek him.
(Lam. 3.22 − 25)

Now turn to page 13

Option 2. *Psalm* 46

1. God is our refuge and strength:
   a very present help in trouble.

2. Therefore we will not fear, though the earth be moved:
   and though the mountains are shaken in the midst of the sea;

3. though the waters rage and foam:
   and though the mountains quake at the rising of the sea.

4. The Lord of hosts is with us:
   the God of Jacob is our stronghold.

5. 'Be still, and know that I am God:
   I will be exalted among the nations, I will be exalted
      upon the earth.'

6. The Lord of hosts is with us:
   the God of Jacob is our stronghold.

   Glory to the Father . . .

It is not ourselves that we proclaim; we proclaim Christ Jesus as
Lord, and ourselves as your servants for Jesus' sake. For the same
God who said, 'Out of darkness let light shine,' has caused his light
to shine within us, to give the light of revelation – the revelation of
the glory of God in the face of Jesus Christ. (2 Cor. 4.5 – 6)

Now turn to page 13

Option 3. *Psalm* 63

1. O God you are my God:
   eagerly will I seek you.

2. My soul thirsts for you, my flesh longs for you:
   as a dry and thirsty land where no water is.

3. So it was when I beheld you in the sanctuary:
   and saw your power and your glory.

4. For your unchanging goodness is better than life:
   therefore my lips shall praise you.

5. And so I will bless you as long as I live:
   and in your name will I lift my hands on high.

6. My longing shall be satisfied as with marrow and fatness:
   my mouth shall praise you with exultant lips.

   Glory to the Father . . .

Live like those who are at home in daylight, for where light is, there all goodness springs up, all justice and truth. Everything, when once the light has shown it up, is illumined, and everything thus illumined is all light. And so the hymn says: 'Awake, sleeper, rise from the dead, and Christ will shine upon you.' (Eph. 5/9,13,14)

Now turn to page 13

Option 4. *Psalm* 145

1. Your kingdom is an everlasting kingdom:
    and your dominion endures through all generations.

2. The Lord upholds all those who stumble:
    and raises up those that are bowed down.

3. The eyes of all look to you in hope:
    and you give them their food in due season;

4. You open wide your hand:
    and fill all things living with your bounteous gift.

5. The Lord is just in all his ways:
    and faithful in all his dealings.

6. The Lord is near to all who call upon him:
    to all who call upon him in truth.

    Glory to the Father . . .

Come, let us return to the Lord; for he has torn us and will heal us,
he has struck us and he will bind up our wounds; after two days he
will revive us, on the third day he will restore us, that in his presence
we may live. Let us humble ourselves, let us strive to know the Lord,
whose justice dawns like morning light, and its dawning is as sure as
the sunrise. It will come to us like a shower, like spring rains that
water the earth. (Hosea 6.1 – 3)

III. CANTICLE AND PRAYER

Benedictus

1. Blessed be the Lord the God of Israel:
   for he has come to his people and set them free.

2. He has raised up for us a mighty saviour:
   born of the house of his servant David.

3. Through his holy prophets he promised of old:
   that he would save us from our enemies,
       from the hands of all that hate us.

4. He promised to show mercy to our fathers:
   and to remember his holy covenant.

5. This was the oath he swore to our father Abraham:
   to set us free from the hands of our enemies,

6. free to worship him without fear:
   holy and righteous in his sight all the days of our life.

7. You my child shall be called the prophet of the most high:
   for you will go before the Lord to prepare his way,

8. to give his people knowledge of salvation:
   by the forgiveness of all their sins.

9. In the tender compassion of our God:
   the dawn from on high shall break upon us,

10. to shine on those who dwell in darkness
       and the shadow of death:
    and to guide our feet into the way of peace.

   Glory to the Father . . .

Silence or words

Kyrie

> Lord have mercy upon us.
> Christ have mercy upon us.
> Lord have mercy upon us.

Lord's Prayer

> Our Father in heaven,
> hallowed be your name,
> your kingdom come,
> your will be done, on earth as in heaven.
> Give us today our daily bread.
> Forgive us our sins
> as we forgive those who sin against us.
> Do not bring us to the time of trial
> but deliver us from evil.
> For the kingdom, the power and the glory
> are yours, now and for ever. **Amen.**

Collect

God most holy, we give you thanks for bringing us out of the shadow of night into the light of morning; and we ask you for the joy of spending this day in your service, so that when evening comes, we may once more give you thanks, through Jesus Christ, your Son, our Lord. **Amen.**

the grace.

14

hymn.

ETERNAL REST GRANT UNTO THEM
O LORD, AND LET LIGHT PERPETUAL

Evening Prayer

I. INVOCATION

V O God, make speed to save us;
R O Lord, make haste to help us.

Glory to the Father, and to the Son, and to the Holy Spirit:
as it was in the beginning is now, and shall be for ever. **Amen.**

Now turn to pages 16, 17, 18, 19, 20, 21, 22, 23 *or* 24, *according to the season.*

II. PSALMODY AND SCRIPTURE

Advent (Anticipation)

Psalm 75

1. We give you thanks, O God, we give you thanks:
   we call upon your name and tell of all the wonders
       you have done.

2. 'I will surely appoint a time:
   when I, the Lord, will judge with equity.

3. 'Though the earth shake and all who dwell in it:
   it is I that have founded its pillars.

4. 'I will say to the boasters, "Boast no more:
   or speak so proud and stifl-necked".'

5. For there is none from the east or from the west:
   or from the wilderness who can raise up;

6. But it is God who is the judge:
   who puts down one and exalts another.

   Glory to the Father . . .

May the God of peace himself sanctify you wholly; and may your spirit and soul and body be kept sound and blameless at the coming of our Lord Jesus Christ. He who calls you is faithful and he will do it. (1 Thess. 5.23 – 24)

Now turn to page 25

Christmas (Incarnation)

Psalm 113

1. Praise the Lord, O sing praises you that are his servants:
   O praise the name of the Lord.

2. Let the name of the Lord be blessed:
   from this time forward and for ever.

3. From the rising of the sun to its going down:
   let the name of the Lord be praised.

4. The Lord is exalted over all the nations:
   and his glory is above the heavens.

5. Who can be likened to the Lord our God:
   in heaven or upon the earth,

6. who has his dwelling so high:
   yet condescends to look on things beneath ?

7. He raises the lowly from the dust:
   and lifts the poor from out of the dungheap;

8. he gives them a place among the princes:
   even among the princes of his people.

9. He causes the barren woman to keep house:
   and makes her a joyful mother of children. Praise the Lord.

   Glory to the Father . . .

When the time had fully come, God sent forth his Son, born of
woman, born under the law, to redeem those who were under the
law, so that we might receive adoption as sons. (Gal. 4.4 – 5)

Now turn to page 25

Lent (Returning to God)

Psalm 130

1. Out of the depths have I called to you, O Lord:
   Lord, hear my voice.

2. O let your ears consider well:
   the voice of my supplication.

3. If you, Lord, should note what we do wrong:
   who then, O Lord, could stand?

4. But there is forgiveness with you:
   so that you shall be feared.

5. I wait for the Lord, my soul waits for him:
   and in his word is my hope.

6. My soul looks for the Lord:
   more than watchmen for the morning, more, I say, than
      watchmen for the morning.

7. O Israel, trust in the Lord, for with the Lord there is mercy:
   and with him is ample redemption.

8. He will redeem Israel:
   from the multitude of his sins.

   Glory to the Father . . .

Do you not know that in a race all the runners compete, but only one receives the prize? So run that you may obtain it. Every athlete exercises self-control in all things. They do it to receive a perishable wreath, but we an imperishable. (1 Cor. 9.24 – 25)

Now turn to page 25

Easter (Resurrection)

Psalm 114

1. When Israel came out of Egypt:
   and the house of Jacob from among a people
         of an alien tongue,

2. Judah became his sanctuary:
   and Israel his dominion.

3. The sea saw that, and fled:
   Jordan was driven back.

4. The mountains skipped like rams:
   and the little hills like young sheep.

5. What ailed you, O sea, that you fled:
   O Jordan, that you were driven back?

6. You mountains, that you skipped like rams:
   and you little hills like young sheep?

7. Tremble, O earth, at the presence of the Lord:
   at the presence of the God of Jacob,

8. Who turned the rock into a pool of water:
   and the flint-stone into a welling spring.

   Glory to the Father . . .

But God, who is rich in mercy, out of the great love with which he loved us, even when we were dead through our trespasses, made us alive together with Christ (by grace you have been saved), and raised us up with him, and made us sit with him in the heavenly places in Christ Jesus. (Eph. 2.4 – 6)

Now turn to page 25

Ascension to Pentecost (Fulfilment)

Psalm 23

1. The Lord is my shepherd:
   therefore can I lack nothing,

2. He will make me lie down in green pastures:
   and lead me beside still waters.

3. He will refresh my soul:
   and guide me in right pathways for his name's sake.

4. Though I walk through the valley of the shadow of death,
        I will fear no evil:
   for you are with me, your rod and staff comfort me.

5. You spread a table before me in the face of those
        who trouble me:
   you have anointed my head with oil, and my cup will be full.

6. Surely your goodness and loving-kindness will follow me
        all the days of my life:
   and I shall dwell in the house of the Lord for ever.

   Glory to the Father . . .

If the Spirit of him who raised Jesus from the dead dwells in you, he who raised Christ Jesus from the dead will give life to your mortal bodies also through his Spirit which dwells in you. (Rom. 8.11)

Now turn to page 25

Other days

Option 1. *Psalm* 103

1. Praise the Lord O my soul:
    and all that is within me praise his holy name.

2. Praise the Lord O my soul:
    and forget not all his benefits,

3. Who forgives all your sin:
    and heals all your infirmities,

4. Who redeems your life from the Pit:
    and crowns you with mercy and compassion;

5. Who satisfies your being with good things:
    so that your youth is renewed like an eagle's.

6. Praise the Lord all his works
       in all places of his dominion:
    praise the Lord O my soul!

    Glory to the Father . . .

Come to me, all whose work is hard, whose load is heavy; and I will give you relief. Bend your necks to my yoke, and learn from me, for I am gentle and humble-hearted, and your souls will find relief. For my yoke is good to bear, my load is light. (Mt. 11.28 – 30)

Now turn to page 25

Option 2. *Psalm* 111

1. O praise the Lord. I will praise the Lord with my whole heart:
   in the company of the upright and among the congregation.

2. The works of the Lord are great:
   and studied by all who delight in them.

3. His marvellous acts have won him a name to be remembered:
   the Lord is gracious and merciful.

4. He gives food to those who fear him:
   he remembers his covenant for ever.

5. He sent redemption to his people, he ordained
         his covenant for ever:
   holy is his name and worthy to be feared.

6. The fear of the Lord is the beginning of wisdom, and of good
         understanding are those that keep his commandments:
   his praise shall endure for ever.

   Glory to the Father . . .

O the depths of the riches and wisdom and knowledge of God!
How unsearchable are his judgements and how inscrutable his
ways! 'For who has known the mind of the Lord, or who has
been his counsellor? Or who has given a gift to him that he
might be repaid?' For from him and to him are all things. To
him be glory for ever. (Rom. 11.33 − 36)

Now turn to page 25

Option 3. *Psalm* 139

1. O Lord you have searched me out and known me:
   you know when I sit or when I stand,
       you comprehend my thoughts long before.

2. Such knowledge is too wonderful for me:
   so high that I cannot endure it.

3. If I spread out my wings towards the morning:
   or dwell in the uttermost parts of the sea,

4. even there your hand shall lead me:
   and your right hand shall hold me.

5. If I say 'Surely the darkness will cover me:
   and the night will enclose me',

6. the darkness is no darkness with you
       but the night is as clear as the day:
   the darkness and the light are both alike.

   Glory to the Father . . .

Do not store up for yourselves treasure on earth, where it grows
rusty and moth-eaten, and thieves break in to steal it. Store up
treasure in heaven, where there is no moth and no rust to spoil it, no
thieves to break in and steal. For where your treasure is, there will
your heart be also. (Mt. 6.19 – 21)

Now turn to page 25

Option 4. *Psalm* 147

1. O praise the Lord
      for it is a good thing to sing praises to our God:
   and to praise him is joyful and right.

2. The Lord is rebuilding Jerusalem:
   he is gathering together the scattered outcasts of Israel.

3. He heals the broken in spirit:
   and binds up their wounds.

4. Great is our Lord and great is his power:
   there is no measuring his understanding.

5. Praise the Lord O Jerusalem:
   sing praises to your God O Zion.

6. For he has strengthened the bars of your gates:
   and blessed your children within you.

   Glory to the Father . . .

The kingdom of God is like the mustard-seed, which is smaller than
any seed in the ground at its sowing. But once sown, it springs up
and grows taller than any other plant, and forms branches so large
that the birds can settle in its shade. (Mk. 4.31f)

24

III. CANTICLE AND PRAYER

Magnificat

1. My soul proclaims the greatness of the Lord:
      my spirit rejoices in God my Saviour;

2. for he has looked with favour on his lowly servant:
   from this day all generations will call me blessed;

3. the Almighty has done great things for me:
   and holy is his name.

4. He has mercy on those who fear him:
   in every generation.

5. He has shown the strength of his arm:
   he has scattered the proud in their conceit.

6. He has cast down the mighty from their thrones:
   and has lifted up the lowly.

7. He has filled the hungry with good things:
   and the rich he has sent away empty.

8. He has come to the help of his servant Israel:
   for he has remembered his promise of mercy,

9. the promise he made to our fathers:
   to Abraham and his children for ever.

Glory to the Father . . .

Silence or words

Kyrie

Lord have mercy upon us.
Christ have mercy upon us.
Lord have mercy upon us.

Lord's Prayer

Our Father in heaven,
hallowed be your name,
your kingdom come,
your will be done, on earth as in heaven.
Give us today our daily bread.
Forgive us our sins
as we forgive those who sin against us.
Do not bring us to the time of trial
but deliver us from evil.
For the kingdom, the power and the glory
are yours, now and for ever. **Amen.**

Collect

Lord, God almighty, come and dispel the darkness from our hearts,
that in the radiance of your brightness we may know you, the only
unfading light, glorious in all eternity. **Amen.**